THE MOON OF THE
DEER

THE THIRTEEN MOONS

The Moon of the Owls (JANUARY)

The Moon of the Bears (FEBRUARY)

The Moon of the Salamanders (MARCH)

The Moon of the Chickarees (APRIL)

The Moon of the Monarch Butterflies (MAY)

The Moon of the Fox Pups (JUNE)

The Moon of the Wild Pigs (JULY)

The Moon of the Mountain Lions (AUGUST)

The Moon of the Deer (SEPTEMBER)

The Moon of the Alligators (OCTOBER)

The Moon of the Gray Wolves (NOVEMBER)

The Moon of the Winter Bird (DECEMBER)

The Moon of the Moles (DECEMBER–JANUARY)

NEW EDITION   THE THIRTEEN MOONS

THE MOON OF THE
DEER

BY JEAN CRAIGHEAD GEORGE

ILLUSTRATED BY SAL CATALANO

HarperCollins*Publishers*

The illustrations in this book were prepared
with mixed media: acrylic paints, opaque tempera,
and pastels on paper board.

The Moon of the Deer
Text copyright © 1969, 1992 by Jean Craighead George
Illustrations copyright © 1992 by Sal Catalano

Typography by Al Cetta
1 2 3 4 5 6 7 8 9 10
NEW EDITION

Library of Congress Cataloging-in-Publication Data
George, Jean Craighead, date
   The moon of the deer / Jean Craighead George ; illustrated by
Sal Catalano.—New ed.
      p.   cm. — (The Thirteen moons)
   Summary: A young buck weathers a hurricane that strikes the
coast of Connecticut in September.
   ISBN 0-06-020261-0. — ISBN 0-06-020262-9 (lib. bdg.)
   1. Deer—Juvenile literature.   2. White-tailed deer—
Connecticut—Juvenile Literature.   [1. White-tailed
deer.   2. Deer.]   I. Catalano, Sal, ill.   II. Title.   III. Series:
George, Jean Craighead, date, Thirteen moons (HarperCollins)
QL795.D3G4   1992   91-14607
599.73′57—dc20   CIP
                                                                AC r91

Why is this series called The Thirteen Moons?

Each year there are either thirteen full moons or thirteen new moons. This series of books is named in their honor.

Our culture, which bases its calendar year on sun-time, has no names for the thirteen moons. I have named the thirteen lunar months after thirteen North American animals. Primarily night prowlers, these animals, at a particular time of the year in a particular place, do wondrous things. The places are known to you, but the animal moon names are not because I made them up. So that you can place them on our sun calendar, I have identified them with the names of our months. When I ran out of these, I gave the thirteenth moon, the Moon of the Moles, the expandable name December-January.

Fortunately, the animals do not need calendars, for names or no names, sun-time or moon-time, they follow their own inner clocks.

—JEAN CRAIGHEAD GEORGE

THE FULL MOON of September rose at a few minutes past six in the evening. The huge orange globe, which seemed to be lit from within, was called the Harvest Moon, the moon of the autumnal equinox. It came up as the sun went down, a phenomenon that gives farmers extra light by which to harvest their crops before the killing frost comes.

For the young males of the white-tailed deer, the all-night moon was the moon of challenge.

Across southern Canada, the United States,

and Mexico (with the exception of California, Nevada, and Utah), the one-and-a-half-year-old bucks were each sporting two daggerlike antlers. They snorted as they sharpened them on trees and bushes. Challenges were ahead.

One of these young bucks was a resident of Mamacoke Marsh, on the Connecticut shore. Golden-gray in color with large, heavily lashed eyes, he stood in the moonlight on a wooded hill above his span of the tidal marshes. Beyond the marshes stretched the bay and, farther out to sea, the barrier islands.

The young buck was looking down on the continent's end. Here the sea mingled with rippling grasses to make one of the earth's most valuable natural resources. Like all salt marshes, it was a nursery for ocean fish and a food source for the vast variety of life that lives in the estuaries and bays.

At midnight the young buck was resting in the groundsel-tree patch and chewing his cud. Like all deer, he was usually abroad only in the dawn and twilight, but the constant light from the Harvest Moon permitted him to wander from moonrise to moonset. The sound of heavy hoofbeats alerted him. An enormous buck was coming his way. The young buck's long, sensitive nose, which could pick up at least a million odors we will never know, tingled with the zestful scent of the eight-pointer, the largest and most aggressive white-tailed deer in the Mamacoke Marsh.

The marsh seemed an unlikely home for deer, with its tides and salt water; but it was, in fact, an Eden for the deer. Just behind the beach grew a seaside garden of wildflowers—sea lavender, purple gerardia, seaside goldenrod and salt-wort—that the deer grazed in summer and early

September. On higher and drier soil grew the salt-meadow grass and cordgrass, rich in minerals and vitamins. Even higher grew the switch grass, whose seeds the deer ate. At the land side of the tidal marsh, elder bushes and groundsel trees gave shelter and browse to the deer. Westward of this community of plants stood the oak woods, and beyond them the pines. The marsh was home not only to the deer, but to sparrows, shorebirds, geese, muskrats, raccoons, and otters. It fed millions of shorebirds, geese, and ducks as they migrated back and forth from their breeding to their wintering grounds.

The tempo of the hoofbeats in the groundsel trees increased. The eight-point buck was trotting the young buck's way. The young buck felt the challenge of his new antlers and walked forward to meet him. The older buck grunted a warning. The young one hesitated. Then he moved into the cordgrass and stopped.

The world at his feet was teeming with insects, crabs, snails, spiders, birds, and worms, for the cordgrass nourishes most of the life in the marsh. When the tide comes in, tons of plant minerals dissolve in the water. As it goes out, the minerals and organic material fertilize the channels and estuaries as well as the bays and ocean. Tidal marshes produce ten times as much food as any comparable area on land—fish, scallops, blue crabs, quahogs, and soft-shell clams, by the millions of tons. The white-tailed deer herd of Mamacoke Marsh had inherited a wealthy land.

The groundsel trees cracked, and the magnificent head and antlers of the old buck were thrust into view. They gleamed in the moonlight. In seeming madness, the young buck lowered his head in challenge. His little spikes shone like silver daggers. They had begun to bud in April

and had grown all summer under a soft skin called velvet. By early September the spikes were hard and fully developed. Only a few days ago the spike buck had scratched the last tag of velvet from one spike and had polished them both on the trunk of a tree. Now he had turned from a gentle browser into a fighting warrior. He had charged the trees and chased the sea gulls. He had pawed the ground. He had run thirty-five miles an hour, jumped thirty feet horizontally, and leaped eight and a half feet in the air. He had rushed up to meet other spike bucks, lowered his head, and clanked weapons with them halfheartedly. They were still adolescents and not eager to fight.

The rutting, or mating, season was a month away. From late October through February, the older bucks would battle with their antlers to win and then protect their harems, female deer. They began this ritual in September by chasing off the spike bucks. The young bucks were easy to conquer. The spike buck of Mamacoke Marsh was a case in point. The old buck stepped out of the groundsel trees. The spike buck lowered his head to challenge him. The monarch snorted and tossed his huge rack. The sound and sight of the eight-point buck ended the battle. The young buck ran, the white fur under his lifted tail flashing the signal "run, danger." The eight-point buck jogged back into the groundsel trees; but not far.

The spike buck recovered from his scare in the tall cordgrass, which almost reached his shoulders. When he had calmed down, he lowered his head and cropped the seeds. Although he didn't know it, he was meeting another September challenge. His body was demanding a diet that would prepare him for winter—seeds, nuts, fruits, and the twigs of vitamin-rich bushes and trees. Earlier this evening he had smelled hawthorns and sumac inland, but now he dared not pass the eight-point buck to find them. He settled for the seeds of the marsh grasses and the protection of their tall stems.

Several days later the sun rose behind swirling clouds. The spike buck stopped browsing and went to his day bed in the cordgrass. He had not been back to the groundsel trees since the buck had warned him away.

A clapper rail slipped past him and ran into the groundsel tree patch. This was unusual, for the long-necked, slender bird lived far out in the marshes. The spike buck had never seen her anywhere but in the sweet salt-meadow grass and among the reeds and rushes along the tidal channels.

The spike buck could smell her fear. He lifted his head to find her reason for flight. A flock of red-winged blackbirds swept over, around him,

and into the groundsel trees. They alighted on the twisted limbs without a sound. Their silence was unusual. Since the crescent moon of September, these birds had been gathering in the marsh by the noisy thousands. They were flocking together in preparation for their fall migration to the southern states. Their silent flight this morning alerted the young buck. The birds often saw enemies before he did. He listened for the sounds of humans.

There were none. The wide, flat marsh was deathly quiet. Even the gulls were not crying as they awakened. The cicadas in the oak forest that usually sang with earsplitting volume in September were silent. The crickets did not rasp their wings together as usual, and the miles of yellowing grass and reeds did not swish.

The spike buck began to feel physically uncomfortable. The atmospheric pressure was dropping. The weight of the air was much less than the normal fifteen pounds per square inch. It was down to twelve pounds per square inch, and affecting his ears and body.

He started back to the groundsel trees, remembered the eight-point buck, and retreated to the edge of a channel that ran out to sea. The tide was low, very low.

A soft rain began to fall. Nearby, a flock of Canada geese gabbled nervously and clustered together. They usually ignored rain, but this morning the atmospheric pressure was making them wary. The birds had left Maine yesterday morning, flying in a V and *honk-a-lonk*ing to keep together. They had arrived at Mamacoke Marsh at dusk. Twenty-five strong, the flock had settled in to rest and eat for a few days before going on down the coast. They would follow the tidal marshes that stretch from Connecticut to

Georgia, and overwinter on the ponds, lakes, and marshes in the Southeastern and Gulf states.

More knowledgeable about atmospheric pressure than the inexperienced deer, they began moving inland.

Their nervous gabbling made the spike buck uneasy. He sniffed, twitched his ears, and looked around to better understand their message. No telltale scents came from the land, and no breeze blew off the ocean. He lifted his head. There was no wind at all. Then his senses told him what the birds already knew; a storm was coming. But this was not one of summer's thunderstorms, it was one of September's wild and devastating hurricanes. Born over the tropical ocean, it had gathered strength as it came up the coast over water. Now it was headed for landfall on Connecticut's shore. The pressure dropped lower.

The spike buck turned away from the sea and

ran for his groundsel patch, despite the big buck.

As he approached, twigs snapped, and the eight-point buck stepped out into view. In the darkness, his rack loomed black, his nostrils flared. He lowered his antlers—a challenge to fight. The spike buck accepted, lowered his head, and flaunted his spikes. The older buck charged.

When the big hoofs thundered against the ground, the spike buck knew what to do. He turned and sped toward the ocean. White flag up, he bolted across the meadow in twenty-foot bounds, thrashing the seed-filled grass heads wherever his feet went down. The seaside goldenrod nodded in the wind he made.

He ran until he could go no farther. He was on the dunes at the end of the marsh. Beyond boomed heavy storm waves. Shivering, he turned around and walked back to the green reeds where the seaside sparrows made their nests in the spring.

The buck had filled him with fear, but the sight of the marsh was even more terrifying. The channel was almost empty of water, and its muddy bottom gleamed like metal in the stillness. A new kind of enemy was challenging him. He lay down in the reeds to hide from the danger as his mother had taught him to do when he was a fawn.

The drizzle turned to rain. The stillness became more and more ominous. Finally fatigue overcame him, and he tucked his head on his haunch and slept. Around noon he was awakened by a crackling sound in the channel below the reeds. The thousands of fiddler crabs that lived in holes in the bank were noisily blowing and breaking bubbles. The tide had been out so long, they were circulating the water in their mouths to absorb its oxygen and stay alive.

The sea water was far, far out. The low

pressure of the hurricane had sucked the water out of the marsh channels and up into the center of the storm, just as liquid is drawn up in a straw when it's sucked on. The column of water in the low-pressure area was a tidal wave—and it was moving landward. As it neared Mamacoke Marsh, the wind started blowing. The rain deluged the coast. The crabs bubbled and snapped. Droves of wildlife abandoned the marsh, and the spike buck once more started back to the groundsel trees. As he neared the sheltered spot, his fear of the monarch stopped him again.

A lone sandpiper ran across the empty channel flats. The bird was not behaving right. It searched and stopped too much, turned around and flicked its wings too frequently. A young bird, it had been running the shores with its parents since June. With the coming of September, the family had flocked with other sandpiper families. Every day they hunted the beaches for sand crabs and sand fleas, then flew out over the ocean and came back. They were warming up for their migration to the Gulf Coast in October.

This morning the lone bird had set out to sea to exercise his wings again. The other sandpipers had not followed. Sensing the coming storm, they had flown up the channel, over the groundsel trees and oaks, and far beyond the pines. When the lone bird returned, he alighted on a deserted beach. He ran, stopped, flicked his wings, and called. Suddenly he screamed his alarm call and flew into the wind.

The cry warned the spike buck. Sensing that he too must act, but afraid to go home, he ran to the edge of the channel. He would swim across to the woods on the other shore; however, there was no water, so he could not swim. He hesitated, for he knew from experience the hazards of the mire on the bottom of the channel. He had sunk up to his ankles in it once. As he stood in the rain, bubbles popped on the surface of the mud as razor-edged and quahog clams burrowed down deep. Their disappearance was not unusual, for each fall they migrated downward to avoid the cold. It was their haste that was alarming. Too many bubbled too frantically. They were traveling rapidly into the mud to get below the scouring action of the storm waves.

The mussels in the channels had sewn themselves to rocks and to one another with threads of tough mucus, spun from their hidden mouths. This was quite normal. But it was not normal that they were now swiftly spinning even more threads to bind themselves more securely to their moorings.

The spike buck was afraid of the mire and once more started back to the groundsel trees. Again, fear of the eight-point buck overwhelmed him. He walked out to the dunes and into the saltwater grass, one of the plants to grow nearest to the sea. Life is harsh on the beach: The wind blows constantly, soils are poor, and the water is salty. Yet saltwater grass manages to survive these rigors. Its thick leaves hold fresh water as the desert's cacti do. Its roots are shallow and numerous to absorb what little nutrition there is in the sand.

The deer cropped a few watery leaves and lay down. Head up, ears twitching, he let his nose sort out the myriad odors on the wind.

A gull screamed its alarm cry. The grasses whipped and flattened. On land, telephone poles snapped and trees fell. Roofs flew off houses. Then, out beyond the dunes, an ominous roar began. The tidal wave was coming in. On it rode living miles of little fish that had been drawn

from the channel and were now riding back to the marsh. The full force of the hurricane was about to strike Mamacoke Marsh.

The spike buck ran inland before the roar. The wind shoved him along. Overhead the lonely sandpiper cried once, then cried no more.

The spike buck came back to the channel edge. He could not go home, and he could not stay. He had no choice but to try to cross the mud flats to the woods south of his groundsel-tree home.

The deer's small cloven hoofs were not designed to walk on mud like the broad hoofs of his bog relative, the moose. Before he had gone many steps, he began to sink. Struggling to free himself, he only sank deeper.

A black duck came running across the mud flat. He was hurrying inland by the easiest route, the waterless channel. Not seeing the buck in the torrential rain, he crashed into him, flapped his wings, and ran up the bank into the reeds.

The spike buck fought to extricate his feet from the mud until he was exhausted. Laying his chin upon the black channel mire, he rested. As he did, calmness and strength returned to him.

Carefully he pulled one front leg out of the mire and stretched it out. Then he eased the other out and, spreading them both as a swimmer would, made himself more buoyant. He did not sink again, but he could not make progress with his legs splayed out.

The wind was now gusting at eighty miles an hour. It was strong enough to blow him away and break his legs if he stood up. Being flat turned out to be a lifesaver. He was so low, he was safe. While the winds raged above him, he pulled his hind legs out of the mud.

With a growl the tidal wave struck the marsh, lifted the young buck up, and carried him land-

ward. In mere seconds he was tossed into the groundsel trees. With him rode driftwood, seaweed, shells and reeds, fish and dead birds.

The spike buck got to his feet and climbed up the groundsel knoll heading for the oak ridge, the highest ground for miles. Even his fear of the eight-point buck no longer held him back. The water was swirling in behind him.

Mice and muskrats deserted their homes in the marsh and scurried up the hill with him. Snakes climbed trees, and raccoons swam toward the forest. Songbirds flew to limbs on the lee side of tree trunks. They shook themselves to keep the driving rain from soaking their feathers.

The young buck reached the top of the groundsel knoll. As tired as he was, he was prepared to fight the eight-point buck. He listened and smelled. Not a deer was anywhere. Trees snapped and bent in the wind, but his herd

was gone. They had run inland and were waiting out the storm in a valley in the pine forest.

As the wind and rain raged on, the young buck turned and faced into the hurricane. Sticks flew through the air; the dry elderberries of September hit his nose like darts. He shifted his weight from one hind leg to the other. Late in the afternoon he lay down, but not with any great sense of security. The ocean was still rising. It covered the switch grass and climbed into the groundsel patch—and kept coming.

When the waves lapped his feet, he ran for higher ground in the oak forest. But he did not go far. On the other side of the groundsel knoll the strange new sea boiled. The knoll was surrounded and would soon be under water. Easing into the flood, he began to swim. Once he touched ground, only to be lifted by a swell and washed back to the groundsel trees. He started off again.

Swimming, fighting to survive, the spike buck rode the next swell into the oaks. He dug in his hoofs and frantically climbed to the top of the ridge. There he collapsed and rested. Suddenly the rain stopped, the winds ceased. The sun came out. Mamacoke Marsh was calm and beautiful. The eye of the hurricane had arrived.

He closed his eyelids and slept while the eye of the storm passed, and the rain and wind began again. The southern side of the hurricane was not as violent, and the spike buck slept through it.

Before sunset the next evening, the young buck returned to the marsh. The wind-beaten grasses and reeds had sprung back, and gulls flew overhead hunting the fish that had been stranded on land by the tidal wave. The muskrats were back mending their lodges; the red-winged blackbirds were calling and wheeling up and over the channels. The geese were *honk-a-lonk*ing.

Life in the tidal marshes has adapted over the millennia to the ravages of sea and storm and wind. Everything was back to normal.

A zestful odor reached the nose of the spike buck. He turned his head. The eight-point buck was coming toward him, his rack spanning thirty-three inches. Once more the young buck ran to the dunes, his white tail flag flying and twitching.

Another year would pass before he would challenge the monarch again. By then he would have shed his spikes in February, and started growing new ones in April. These would branch into antlers with one or two points. As each year passed, they would grow until he carried a great rack like the monarch's. Then he would fight the old buck and win. His fawns would romp in the grasses of Mamacoke Marsh, and his own spike bucks would run from his challenges in September.

The buck walked far down the dunes, then turned inland to another patch of groundsel trees. Here he would wait until the rut was over, and he and the monarch could live in peace. Then he and his herd would trek to the valley in the pines to yard during the ice and snow storms of winter.

The spike buck had met the challenge of the September moon. He probably would live to see sixteen more, for the first year and a half of a deer's life are the hardest. He chewed his cud and watched the moon rise as the sun went down.

Bibliography

Adler, C.S. *Carly's Buck.* New York: Clarion Books, 1987.

Ahlstrom, Mark E. *The Whitetail.* Riverside, NJ: Crestwood House, 1983.

Arnosky, Jim. *Deer at the Brook.* New York: Lothrop, Lee & Shepard Company, 1985.

Bailey, Jill. *Discovering Deer.* New York: The Bookwright Press, 1988.

Burt, William H. and Richard P. Grossenheider. *A Field Guide to the Mammals.* The Peterson Field Guide Series. Boston: Houghton Mifflin Company, 1976.

Carner, Chas., *Tawny.* New York: The Macmillan Company, 1978.

Carrick, Donald. *Harald and the Great Stag.* New York: Clarion Books, 1988.

Gamlin, Linda. *The Deer in the Forest.* Milwaukee, WI: Stevens Publishers, 1988.

LaBastille, Anne. *Whitetailed Deer.* Vienna, VA: National Wildlife Federation, 1977.

McClung, Robert M. *Whitetail.* New York: William Morrow and Company, Inc., 1987.

Palmer, Ralph S. *The Mammal Guide.* Garden City, NY: Doubleday & Company, 1954.

Paulsen, Gary. *Tracker.* New York: Bradbury Press, 1984.

Rawlings, Marjorie Kinnan. *The Yearling.* New York: Charles Scribner's Sons, 1985.

Salton, Felix. *Bambi: A Life in the Woods.* New York: Pocket Books, 1988.

Index